MW00883433

THE

WARRIOR

MINDSET

THE
WARRIOR
MINDSET

7 MINDSET SHIFTS TO UNLEASH YOUR INNER WARRIOR

CHITRA ROCHLANI

Published by Happy Self Publishing
www.happyselfpublishing.com
writetous@happyselfpublishing.com

HAPPY
SELF PUBLISHING

Dedicated to the original warrior

MY MOM

Table of Contents

1

Why this book?

Do we really need another book on mindset? After all, haven't the words mindset, and mindfulness been overused by now? We see mindfulness mentioned in books, podcasts, speeches, and even commercials on TV. Every product from pharmaceutical drugs to makeup to kitchen gadgets is promising to help us be more mindful, so that we can find ourselves and our purpose.

Perhaps, but if we have heard so much about it, why do we still struggle to achieve it? Take meditation, for instance. Most people will tell you that they have trouble being consistent mainly because they cannot stop their mind from racing when they try to sit still.

WHY DOES OUR MIND RACE SO MUCH?

1. Because it can! We are capable of producing over 6000 thoughts on any given day.
2. Our thoughts have the ability to transport us back to our memories, past experiences, and into the future where our hopes and dreams lie. So, if each thought can go off on a tangent or multiple tangents, it is no wonder we struggle to get to the proverbial stillness we are all craving.
3. Each of those thoughts has the ability to relive past experiences that have major emotions attached to it. This takes us further down the spiral, and we can get caught in that spiral for days.

The shiny objects we are trying to use to break free from our mind's endless loops don't even begin to go deep let alone help us break out of the deepest depths of our mind. Clearly, there is a big need for clarity and guidance.

We live in a material world, and we did what we were told. We followed the path that was laid out for us. We got the education, the job, the money, the car, the house, the partner, the kids and pets, the technology, the comforts and conveniences this world has to offer. Yet we are more lost than ever.

It is not enough; we want more. This yearning for more comes from the depths of our soul. The loneliness epidemic that is haunting us in a time of hyper-connectivity is proof that we are not where we want to be.

Therefore, if our mind controls most of our lived experiences, it is crucial that we understand it, work on it, and help it find peace. So how do we get there? There are many shiny objects out there in the world. While we can jump from one to another, these so-called shiny objects don't come close to helping us for a few different reasons:

1. Most products or services are not giving us the whole picture. They might be part of the puzzle, but they don't show us the entire journey. For example, a 20-minute meditation session may help me feel calm, but how do I deal with the recurring anger I feel?

2. One size doesn't fit all! This journey is a personal one. What worked for one person may not work for another. If you don't see the direction you need to go in, how do you figure out what works for you? For example, I know people who can clear their mind by serving others in a soup kitchen, but I also know people who attend 10-day spiritual retreats and see no change.

3. They are not holistic. Most of the strategies I have seen are not holistic. Each of them separately may give you a clue into your mindset but struggle to show you the whole picture.

The bottom line is that there is no magic pill, and that's what we're all looking for.

We say we want to be more mindful, and our commercialized world comes up with a product, service, app, or drug that promises to help you be more *you*. They dangle shiny objects, and we jump from one to another thinking the next one will be the magic formula to help us master mindset. We do this with everything: our bodies, our skin, our age, and now we want to do the same with our minds. Let's find the shortest, easiest way to get there.

The problem with this approach is that it is not sustainable. What is the point of feeling extremely Zen in a 20-minute meditation session if you get really annoyed at your teenager the next minute or bubble with rage at the driver that cut you off in traffic later that day? We need to break free of the band-aid mentality and get to the root cause of our problems. We cannot take our deep wounds, slap on a teeny-tiny band aid (no matter how pretty and colorful), and walk around pretending nothing is wrong. It simply doesn't work. And since most of our worldly problems begin with our mindset, we need to start there.

If we're serious about breaking free of the stuff that holds us back, we need to dig deep. This is where this book comes in. My goal with this book is to show you what the journey looks like, help you identify where you are on the path, and give you some steps to rise higher. So, if you're looking for a quick fix or a gimmick to find your Zen then this book is not for you. But if you're in it for the long haul and ready to dig deep, peel the layers of dust covering that beautiful bright spirit of yours, and unleash the warrior within then welcome aboard, my friend. Let's dive right in.

2

Mindset Is Everything

"The mind is a powerful force. It can enslave us or empower us. It can plunge us into the depths of misery or take us to the heights of ecstasy. Learn to use the power wisely."

David Cuschieri

The state of our mind determines the state of our life. Our emotions, feelings, and energy dictate our experiences in life. We see things differently based on how we feel. If we're in a bad mood, we get triggered by things that wouldn't bother us on a good day. On the flip side, if we're having a great day, nothing can bring us down. Every thought we have is a direct result of the mindset we are in at that moment.

If you are in a high-level mindset, you could have nothing and still feel truly blessed beyond measure. You could also be in the most challenging circumstances and stay upbeat. We all know at least one person who has it worse than so many of us and still manages to stay cheerful all the time. For me, it is a friend who makes funny tik-toks about losing her hair to cancer. I also know another person who is always positive despite being a 24/7 caretaker to her special needs child and her sick husband.

If you are in a low-level mindset, you could have millions of dollars in your bank account and still be miserable. Don't we all know someone who has all the beauty, fame, or money in the world but continues to live in fear and insecurity? I know someone who would complain that the bag of money was too heavy even if she won the lottery.

While those are extreme examples, most of us fall somewhere in between. We may not like to admit it, but we have all been victims of a negative mindset. Sometimes, we encounter difficult situations and need to take time to process our feelings. But for the most part, our low-vibe mindset keeps us feeling stuck and becomes an obstacle in our path. Does this mean we should only experience high-level emotions all the time? Not at all.

In fact, we need to feel all the emotions, so we understand what triggers us and why. Knowledge is empowering. It gives us golden insight into our minds and helps us make transformational breakthroughs.

We all react to our experiences differently due to the lens we see things through or due to our past conditioning. The same situation can elicit different reactions in people causing different levels of stress and anxiety. Some people see a homeless man on the street and walk by. Others are so heartbroken that they give him all the money in their wallet, and sit down to talk about how they can get him out of his situation. Similarly, some people get hit with adversity and react with so much grace and dignity while others fall apart.

So, what is the goal of the book? The goal is to get out of this crazy, exhausting roller coaster filled with high-highs and low-lows, and get to a state where we are in charge of our mindset. Where we can handle the curveballs life throws at us with maturity and grace.

Visualization

I want you to take a minute to imagine yourself in full warrior mode. You are ready to tackle anything that life throws at you and know that you can handle it. When life throws you a curveball, you might stumble, but you are able to get right back to your Zen. You know that all your experiences are here to teach you a valuable lesson that is uniquely designed for you.

On the flip side, when something good happens, you enjoy it. But you are also able to stay Zen without letting your ego have a field day. In the process, you quietly inspire those around you. Our mindset has the power to help us make the best out of every situation and stay in a Zen state without going up and down the roller coaster of emotions.

That is the warrior mindset, and that is the goal!

3

But First, A Reality Check

If we truly want to get into a warrior mindset, we need to gain a deep understanding of our mindset and how it works. We need to get real with ourselves—our deepest thoughts and feelings- recognize the thought patterns holding us back from succeeding.

Unfortunately, we have been conditioned to suppress our true feelings and pretend to look perfect, act normal, and hide our problems from the world. We put on a happy face and go about our day in fear that someone might see our vulnerability, and we will look weak, flawed, or incompetent. But why do we put so much pressure on ourselves and deal with this inner struggle every day? Why not just be true to who we are and live an authentic life?

This is driven by one thing—*the quest for perfection*. What's that? The quest for perfection is something we have become hardwired to aim for. We have been taught by our schools, colleges, corporations, media, and society to be perfect in every way possible. We try to get the perfect score on a test, go to the perfect college, get the perfect job, buy the perfect house and car. We are expected to marry the perfect person, raise perfect children (who restart the cycle of perfection), make perfect investments, and be perfect citizens who give back to the community. If all that goes perfectly, we are supposed to plan and execute the perfect retirement, live happily ever after, and leave behind the perfect legacy. When did we buy into this ridiculous idea and let it dominate our entire existence?

Every single media advertisement tries to convince us that we will look, act, and feel perfect after the use of their product or service. We are nothing if not compliant. We hand over the puppet strings of this entire charade into the hands of these marketing agencies and let them pull the strings to make us jump from one shiny object to another.

Here's the problem with perfection. It is simply not sustainable or healthy. It creates a false sense of identity and forces us to be untrue to ourselves. We are probably miserable in our jobs, at home, or in our relationships. We push our true feelings and emotions under the rug and walk around acting like we have everything under control. Meanwhile, the rug gets bumpy and could rip any day. Not only does this cause a lot of inner conflicts, but it also causes a level of isolation that leads to feelings of despair. And since feeling conflicted, lonely, or depressed is frowned upon in our so-called perfect world, we can't even talk about it.

How many of us are lonely, hurt, and depressed on the inside but walk around like everything is in okay? Recent surveys suggest that loneliness is a bigger epidemic than obesity or diabetes. According to the Surgeon General of New York City the impact of loneliness on our health is similar to that of smoking 15 cigarettes a day.

There are many problems with aiming for perfection:

1. It is an endless quest. No matter how much you chase it, perfection keeps getting away.

2. It robs you of the present. When we are busy chasing perfection, we don't stop to savor the success we have achieved so far.
3. It turns you into a harsh critic. Perfectionists are usually harsh critics of themselves and others. This can lead to comparison and competition.
4. It leads to intense insecurity. If you are constantly focused on doing something perfectly, the slightest bit of negative feedback can trigger you to feel inadequate leading to insecurity.
5. It makes us controlling. The quest for perfection makes us check and recheck every move. It kills our intuitive abilities and turns us into controlling taskmasters.

We have believed in the myth of perfection for so long that we have lost our way. Our truth is so heavily masked by our efforts to appear normal that we don't even know where our deep fears, worries, and insecurities take us or where they come from. This leads to lack of authenticity, and frankly, it is exhausting to try and keep up with the facade of perfection. In our attempts to showcase our lives as perfect, we miss out on the opportunity for discovering who we are and what our uniqueness is.

WHAT IS AUTHENTICITY?

Authenticity is when you are united in your thoughts, words, and actions. You are true to yourself and those around you. Since we are so accustomed to being who we are expected to be, we have forgotten who *we* wanted to be. Being authentic requires a lot of inner work because we have to drop the charade of who we pretend to be for the world and connect with wo we are at our core. . We need to get real with ourselves and understand the traits and behaviors we have taken on to impress others. We also have to identify and embrace the traits and behaviors that will help us give back to this world in our unique way.

The amount of energy we spend trying to fit in and be liked is a drain on our system. If we can be brave enough to embrace ourselves truly and completely, we can build the courage to show our authentic selves to the rest of the world. Not only does this free up all that time and energy we spent trying to fit in but also opens us up to attract experiences that fill our cup more.

I want to invite you on a journey of introspection and self-awareness, so you can identify the blind spots in your mindset and release the energy that is being used in trying to be someone you are not. Let's embrace our authenticity and find the courage to share it with the world. You have a unique gift that the world needs. The sooner you find it, the sooner you can give it away.

"The meaning of life is to find your gift. The purpose of life is to give it away."

Pablo Picasso

4

The Witch And The Warrior

The Witch and the Warrior are constantly at war inside our minds. The one who wins is the one we give the megaphone to.

Chitra Rochlani

We all have an inner "witch" and "warrior" who dictate how we feel about ourselves and the world around us. We all know people who seem to be calm in the worst of situations (aka the warriors) and those who fall apart at the simplest of inconveniences (aka the witches). Warriors are not born with their strength, but they become resilient and strong through their experiences. Can you think of some people who may represent warriors? I'm thinking of all the people who beat the odds, show strength in adversity, fight repressing systems, and most of all, understand that they have more power inside them than they like to believe. Maybe you have an inner warrior who dominates in some areas and a witch who dominates in others? Wouldn't you love to embody the warrior mindset in all areas of life?

In order to truly understand how the mind works, we should conduct in-depth research with ourselves and learn about who rules the mind—the witch or the warrior. So, we know how the warrior shows up, but what about the witch? Our inner witch is constantly reminding us of our fears, insecurities, and worries. She loves to make us feel like we are not good enough to achieve our goals and tries to talk us out of dreaming big. Think about a time you were afraid to try something new. Did you hesitate and let the fear win? If you did then you know the witch had a field day because she talked you out of it. The witch is a bully and will always come up when you try to step out of your comfort zone and do something courageous. She will convince you that you are not good enough, and that you should give up on those dreams. Now think about how that made you feel. It is likely that you regret giving up and wish you had persevered and pushed out of your comfort zone.

The warrior, on the other hand, constantly reminds us of our strengths, power, and dreams. She quietly whispers in our ears and nudges us toward our goals and dreams. Think about a time when you acted on a rare moment of courage and achieved something that seemed impossible. How did it feel to go all in and accomplish the scary task? It is likely that you felt a sense of achievement and even experienced a natural high from that accomplishment. How do we make sure that we put the witch in a far corner and hand a megaphone to the warrior, so we can crush this roller coaster called life.

Let's find out together with my 3-step plan to understand when and how the witch and the warrior show up.

Awareness

It is impossible to change any thought, behavior, or habit without first becoming aware of it. The first step is to develop awareness about our inner witch and warrior by observing our daily experiences. We can also look at the people around us and draw inspiration from those living in warrior mode.

It is important to remember that the witch and the warrior are simply two voices in your head. They don't define you. You have the ultimate power over who you listen to, which makes you pretty badass. As you become accustomed to observing your day-to-day experiences through the lens of the witch and the warrior, you may begin to notice who tends to show up more— the witch or the warrior.

Example

My client, Sara, was working with me on her nutrition. One day, she came home from a tough day at work and opened up a box of cookies and ate them all. Once she was done, she felt disgusted and annoyed that she had given in to the craving. As she sent me her daily food log, she shared this experience with me. Clearly, her inner witch was alive and kicking. She felt a lot of shame and guilt about not being able to stick to her meal plan. She beat herself up mentally. When we spoke, I had her share more about her day. As she opened up, we realized that she got triggered at work by her overly demanding boss who made her do all the work but gave the credit to her co-worker, Tom. This made her feel like she was being taken advantage of, and all her extra work was going unnoticed. She was unable to voice her dismay and instead came home looking for something to make her feel good (the sugar-filled, serotonin-inducing cookies).

The cookies provided instant pleasure. But once we figured out the connection between her inability to speak up and her need to feel good about herself, she made a breakthrough. It was no longer a battle of her vs. sugar or willpower but an insight into her triggers. This awareness was huge for her.

ACCEPTANCE

Once the awareness kicks in, you may either feel a sense of relief or a sense of dread. Either way, once you notice the witch and the warrior, it becomes easier to understand who is controlling your actions. One we accept that we tend to get caught up in the witch's evil stories, it becomes easier to create a plan of action. A big part of acceptance is giving yourself some grace and being kind to yourself as you make the transition. If you find that you are in warrior mode, be sure to celebrate that.

Example

Sara became *aware* that it wasn't her lack of willpower, but her need to learn how to voice her concerns and set healthy boundaries that needed attention. And once she saw that pattern, it became easier for her to see that the witch was wrong. She dug a little deeper into her past conditioning and realized that she couldn't speak up because she had always been told to be nice and not say anything that might upset others. Seeing these patterns made it easy for her to accept her situation and give herself some grace through this journey of self-reflection.

ACTION

This is the exciting part. Once you have *awareness* and *acceptance* of your old patterns, it becomes easier to make changes for the future and awaken the warrior within. But before you take a giant leap and crash remember that change can be overwhelming. Your old beliefs didn't become a part of you overnight, and they won't disappear overnight. Change takes time, and it is important to be patient with yourself as you make the transition. I highly recommend that you start with small, baby steps.

Think of a pattern you want to break, start small, and list out some ways you can get the needle moving in the right direction.

Example
For Sara, this meant a few different things. She became aware of her behavior patterns, so we set up sticky notes around her pantry and refrigerator to remind her to pause. She would stop to see if her need for a snack was genuine hunger or a coping mechanism. She also learned to set boundaries and say no if needed, so we came up with a few ways to remind her of why this was important. Finally, she had to speak up when things got out of hand. By taking small steps in the right direction, she began to give voice to the inner warrior and regain her own power at work.

Summary

The witch will always remind us of all our limitations, tell us we are not good enough, and keep us from reaching for our dreams and goals. The warrior, once unleashed, is unstoppable, badass, and cannot be messed with. The warrior is here to remind us of our true purpose, our passion, and the legacy we are meant to leave behind in this world.

Affirmations to bring out your inner warrior.

WITCH
Don't do that. You will make a fool of yourself.

WARRIOR
What if you went for it?

WITCH
Nobody wants to listen to what you have to say.

WARRIOR
I know it's scary, but let's try it.

WITCH
You need to know your limits. I knew you couldn't do it.

WARRIOR
You've gotten through so much; this is nothing. Let's do it.

WITCH
Let's sit here and imagine all the things that could go wrong.

WARRIOR
You are amazing. I know you can do it.

WITCH
You're so (insert negative trait about yourself).
It's no wonder you keep getting stuck.

WARRIOR
You deserve this more than anyone I know.

The journey from the witch to the warrior starts with
empowerment.

MY VERY OWN WARRIOR

My first introduction to mindset came from my mother. My mother is a true warrior and has always displayed a joyous, abundant, optimistic mindset. As a child, I would hear her say that everything happens for a reason. I would challenge her at every step. If a vase broke, I would ask her why the vase broke. What was the reason for that? With a big smile on her face she would say, "So we can finally buy a new one!"

If I complained that I was in pain, she would correct me and say, "You're not in pain. Your foot is in pain. YOU are fine!" I constantly questioned my mother's beliefs, but I was rarely able to win a discussion with her. It was quite annoying as an adolescent, but I realized when I left for college to another country that I had unknowingly adopted her belief system. Her beliefs were helping me cope with the difficult times in my life. I began to look forward to the bright side in every situation. Over the years, I found myself drawn to mindset, psychology, and personal growth, I loved exploring these topics via podcasts, books, seminars, videos, and courses. I knew then that we need to have more conversations around building a strong, empowered, warrior mindset. That was the only way to get to know ourselves and find our purpose in this lifetime.

5

Blessed Not Stressed

Be thankful for what you have. Your life, no matter how bad you think it is, is someone else's fairy tale.

Wale Ayeni

What Is A Stressed Mindset?

A stressed mindset is constantly being in a state of fear, negativity, and worry. If you're stressing about your situation, chances are you are not thinking of solutions or fixes. Although some stress is necessary for us to function. For instance, the stress of getting to work on time helps us plan ahead and get ready, set an alarm, choose the best route to work, etc. Any stress above normal levels is disruptive to our health, relationships, and lives. Have you ever tried to solve a difficult problem from a stressed state of mind? If so, you know that it is very difficult to come up with solutions until you calm yourself and look at the problem from all angles.

What Is A Blessed Mindset?

A blessed mindset is one where no matter what the stressors are in our life, we are able to see past the problem and find the blessing in it. In some dire situations it may be very difficult to find the silver lining, but if you look hard enough, you will find that it could have been a lot worse. This is a source of hope in an otherwise stressful time. Sometimes when it seems impossible to find the blessing, remember that every difficult situation

30

brings with it an opportunity for growth and learning. What can you learn from this experience, and how can you pay it forward? How do we go from a stressed to a blessed mindset?

AWARENESS

As always, the first step is awareness. The minute you catch yourself spiraling out of control in a stressful situation, remind yourself that you are in control of your thoughts, and you can hit the brakes. The first step is to become aware of the thoughts in your mind while you are stressed. It may even help to write down what you're feeling. Sometimes the act of writing it down makes us realize how made-up some of our thoughts are. Stress is usually a result of living in the past or worrying about the future, but if we can hit the brakes and find a way to be mindful of the present, we can curb some of the stress.

Example
Tina was someone who would get stressed easily. While coping with the stress of her job and managing her family and 3 pets, she found out that her mom had been diagnosed with early-stage cancer. This caused her to spiral out of control, and she couldn't stop stressing about all the things that could go wrong. As her mind raced faster than a Ferrari, she realized that it was wreaking havoc on her body. She would get physically sick with thoughts about losing her mom. She realized that she needed to reign it in, so she could actually be there for her mom. This is what awareness looked like for her. It was the first step in changing her mindset.

ACCEPTANCE

How do we create acceptance in the middle of a stressful situation? It is important to note that whether we stress about the situation we are in or not, we will have to deal with the situation and go through it. Once you become aware of your tendency to stress, the next step is to accept that you are a stress-taker. And you want to change that habit, so that you can cope better in future. Any situation only becomes harder when we add stress to it. Stress takes a toll on our ability to reason, intensifies our reaction to the situation, and impacts our mind and body negatively.

Example

In Tina's case, she had to accept that if she didn't take charge of her stress, she would not be able to care for her mom, and her own health would take a hit. She had to accept that she had a tendency to go out of control with her stress. She needed to develop some techniques to cope with difficult situations. Once she accepted this, it gave her the impetus to take action steps toward handling her stress better.

ACTION

The journey from stressed to blessed begins with gratitude. It may seem impossible to be grateful when you are in the middle of a stressful situation, but if you can find even one thing to be grateful for, you will eliminate the stress for those few moments. It is impossible to feel stressed and blessed at the same time. Look around your life, and see what you can be grateful for despite all that seems to be going wrong.

Example

Tina realized no matter how difficult things seemed, there were definitely some silver linings she could acknowledge and feel grateful for. She began making a list and came up with more things than she could imagine. She was thankful that her mother lived close enough, so she could go along on her doctor visits. She was grateful that it was early-stage cancer, her husband was super supportive, her kids were old enough to manage certain tasks, and she had friends who would support her through these tough times. As she began making this list of blessings, she began to feel lighter and filled with hope again.

SUMMARY

Stress is a response that can be controlled. We can train our minds to respond differently when a stressful situation comes our way. Focus on awareness of your triggers, and take inspiration from others who handle the same stress with grace. As you train your mind to see your stress from a different lens, you can build a toolbox to stop the stressful thoughts in their place and bring in gratitude and perspective to replace those thoughts. The more you practice using this toolbox, the easier it gets for you to stay in a blessed mindset.

Affirmations to bring out your inner warrior.

WITCH (STRESSED)
I can't do this; it's too much.

WARRIOR (BLESSED)
I can do this—one step at a time

WITCH (STRESSED)
What if everything goes wrong?

WARRIOR (BLESSED)
What is the best-case scenario?

WITCH (STRESSED)
I can't breathe. I'm drowning in stress.

WARRIOR (BLESSED)
I am not alone. Who can I ask for help?

WITCH
I am STRESSED.

WARRIOR
I am BLESSED.

The journey from stressed to blessed starts with gratitude.

Let's Get to Work

5

4

Feeling BLESSED
in all situations

3

Taking ACTION
and focusing on
gratitude

2

ACCEPTANCE
and willingness to
make changes

1

AWARE or
becoming aware of
stress responses

**THE JOURNEY FROM
STRESSED TO BLESSED**

STRESSED and
frustrated with
its impact

Where do you think you are on the above scale?

List 1 thing that holds you back from being in a blessed mindset?

What is 1 thing you can do to get to a blessed mindset sooner?

What would staying in a blessed mindset do for you?

6

Abundance Not Scarcity

A flower doesn't think of competing with the flowers next to it. It just blooms.

Zen Shin

Our beliefs create our reality. If we believe that there's never enough time, money, or resources then that becomes our reality. If we believe that we are not smart enough, rich enough, or good enough then that defines our reality. If we believe that we will always have an abundance of time, money, and resources then that will become our reality. Abundance doesn't just apply to the material world; it applies to our mindset too. It is important to know if we are in abundance or scarcity.

What Is A Scarcity Mindset?

A scarcity mindset tells you that everything is limited: time, resources, joy, happiness, youth, health, and money. It will ALL run out. The problem with a scarcity mindset is that it has us living in insecurity, doubt, and fear. It has us feeling jealous of others, wishing ill (secretly) on them, and playing (manipulative) games to get ahead. Most of the time, we don't even realize we are doing it. It stops us from being happy for other people's success and showing up authentically because we are too busy living in fear of missing out.

WHAT IS AN ABUNDANT MINDSET?

An abundant mindset tells you that you are exactly where you need to be, experiencing exactly what you need to be experiencing, and learning exactly the lessons you need to be learning. A life lived from an abundant lens means living with gratitude, knowing that the universe has our back, and that there is enough for everyone. An abundant mindset will attract more opportunities and is always open to possibilities. You never have to worry about missing out because you live with the belief that you are being provided with more than you will ever need.

Example

My mother in her ultimate abundant mindset truly believes that she will never have a shortage of money. To this day, she believes that whenever money is running low, she will miraculously find a hidden stash somewhere. For someone who never worked outside the home a single day of her life, she had a lot of confidence in this belief. Sometimes we would be out shopping. On the way back home, she would be looking to pay for the cab and have no money in her wallet only to find a hidden $20 bill at the bottom of her handbag. She didn't live an abundant life by material standards, but her abundant mindset helps her live with ease and flow to this day.

How do we get to this blissful, abundant state? An abundant mindset is more than just about money. It applies to everything we want in life. When we shift our focus to believe that there is enough opportunity, love, and compassion out there for all of us, we elevate our energy and begin to attract more automatically. We begin to collaborate and connect and get rid of the scarce mindset of competition, comparison, and chaos.

The first thing that you need to do to make the journey from scarcity to abundance is to have a strong, unshakeable, firm belief that you will receive everything you deserve. If you don't, there is a lesson in that. To go from scarcity to abundance, we turn to the 3 As.

AWARENESS

Awareness is the first step in making any change. Most people live in a state of scarcity without even realizing it. Some ways that scarcity may show up in our lives are comparison, competition, and complaining. As a result of a scarcity mindset, we hide our success from others and are unable to share in other people's wins. We hide valuable information and resources from others because we feel insecure about sharing them. We hesitate to share our true feelings and isolate ourselves as a result of scarcity.

Example

Jamie was someone who always feared competition. She grew up in a very competitive environment where the other kids in school were constantly trying to get ahead of each other. She learned how to hide information and resources from others to get ahead and continued this behavior in the corporate world. She thought if she did share resources to help others, they would use them and get ahead leaving her behind. Her awareness of her mindset came from attending a group coaching session at work. Someone in the group was struggling with presentations as he could not speak confidently and asked if anyone knew of a resource to help overcome his fear of public speaking. Jamie knew an excellent public speaking coach but hesitated to share the information. Within minutes, she saw 3 other people share information and resources on public speaking. This made her acutely aware of her scarcity mindset. She liked how the energy of the room shifted when everyone was openly sharing information. It became more collaborative, and she wanted to experience more of that.

ACCEPTANCE

As humans, we resist any idea that suggests that we may be flawed. Our society only makes this worse by force-feeding us images of perfection in every aspect of life. We were put on this conveyor belt of success and told that we had to compete with those around us to stay on top. We were taught that for one person to win another has to lose. But instead of looking at our scarcity mindset as a flaw, let's look at it as a clue to the puzzle of who we are. Changing our thoughts and beliefs may be one of the hardest things we do, so let's show ourselves some compassion as we transition from a scarcity mindset to an abundant one. Remember that it is not your fault. You were simply never shown what an abundant mindset looks and feels like.

Example

Jamie knew that hiding information didn't make her feel good, but she also realized that it wasn't her fault that she was acting in this manner. Since childhood, she had been taught to fight for what she needed. At home, she competed with her siblings and at school, with her friends. Overtime, it became an unconscious habit. She accepted that she was struggling with a scarcity mindset, and decided that she was going to make some changes to see how it made her feel.

As Maya Angelou very wisely said, "Do the best you can until you know better. Then when you know better, do better."

ACTION

The hardest part of any change is acceptance of our old behavior. Once you have identified and accepted your scarcity mindset, here are some simple ways to begin.

Gratitude is the cornerstone of abundance. Start by being grateful for what you already have in your life. After that, take a look at all the interactions you have in a day, and see where you can show up with an abundant mindset.

I experienced this recently at a bookstore where I was in line to receive a free copy of a book. They ran out as I got to the front of the line. The store manager asked us to wait as he went to look for more copies in the back. Instead of being disappointed, I joked with the 2 people in line behind me that maybe something better will come. Thereafter, the store manager came back with the last 3 copies of the book, and told us that those were actually signed by the author herself.

One of the biggest reasons to be in an abundant mindset is that it opens us up to unlimited potential. It allows our energy to flow, so that we can attract more. We all have a unique purpose and passion. If we focus on what lights us up, we won't be impacted by what others around us are succeeding at. We might even find joy in lifting others and collaborating with them instead of getting competitive.

Example

For Jamie, she wanted to explore what it felt like to share information freely. She told her coworker about the public speaking coach she had worked with. What she received in return was incredible. Her coworker was so grateful that she shared her gratitude openly with all her friends at work. The public speaking coach was so grateful for the referral that she offered to give Jamie a free session to thank her. The moment you start giving to the world, you open yourself up to receive. Jamie loved how expansive this made her feel, and she continued to share resources with other people at work.

Summary

An abundant mindset is not only a gift to ourselves but to those around us. When you feel abundant, you receive with open arms, you enjoy everything you have, and you give back freely. A scarcity mindset, on the other hand, will always keep us in a state of lack and fear of missing out. Not only will we keep wanting more we will attract more lack into our lives with this energy.

Affirmations to bring out your inner warrior.

WITCH (SCARCITY)
I need to get to it before someone else does.

WARRIOR (ABUNDANCE)
Nobody can take what's mine. My opportunity is waiting for me.

WITCH (SCARCITY)
If I don't reach the goal first, someone else will.

WARRIOR (ABUNDANCE)
The universe has my back and is guiding me to my goal.

WITCH (SCARCITY)
I can't allow myself to fail.

WARRIOR (ABUNDANCE)
There is no failure. Only experience.

WITCH (SCARCITY)
I need to get ahead before I give to others.

WARRIOR (ABUNDANCE)
Let me give what I can, and let's grow together.

WITCH (SCARCITY)
I am SCARCITY.

WARRIOR (ABUNDANCE)
I am ABUNDANCE.

The journey from scarcity to abundance starts with belief.

Let's Get to Work

RATE YOURSELF FROM 1 (SCARCITY) TO 5 (ABUNDANCE)

5

4   ABUNDANCE mode on
(Believing)

3   Taking ACTION and
changing belief

2   ACCEPTANCE and
willingness to make
changes

1   AWARE or becoming
aware of scarcity   **THE JOURNEY FROM SCARCITY
TO ABUNDANCE**

Living in SCARCITY
mindset focused on
lack

Where does scarcity mindset show up for you?

Where do you think you are on the above scale?

List 1 thing that holds you back from being in abundance?

What is 1 thing you can do to get to an abundance mindset?

What would living in abundance do for you?

7

Believer Not
Doubter

Whether you think you can or not, you're right.

Henry Ford

We are all born believers—Every Single One Of Us. Doubt only enters our minds once we experience fear.

WHAT IS A DOUBTER MINDSET?

A doubter mindset is one where we operate from a place of fear and insecurity. We refuse to attempt things and focus on everything that can go wrong if we pursue our dreams. Doubt is the biggest killer of flow and creativity. It kills more dreams than any other obstacle. Self-doubt can lead to low self-confidence and fear of taking chances. Eventually, we stop connecting with our authentic purpose and get stuck living a mediocre, unfulfilled life.

Anytime we think of trying something new and scary, what's the first thing that comes to mind? Self-doubt shows up followed by fear, and we are paralyzed into inaction. While most of us can come up with hundred reasons why we shouldn't do something new and scary, there is one reason why we must defy the odds.

WHAT IS A BELIEVER MINDSET?

A believer mindset is one where we have a strong sense of faith and conviction that we can achieve anything we put our minds to. This strong sense of self is responsible for most of our success. If you ever look at a young child learning to crawl, walk, or run, you will see how strong their self-belief is. They charge forward with an inbuilt desire to succeed and don't stop in fear or self-doubt. That is until we begin to tell them to stop, hold our hand, or think twice before they leap. Children also believe they can be and do anything they want to. Ask a child what he or she wants to be and chances are you will hear something like superman or a rockstar. They truly believe they can do it. They are dreamers and don't believe in self-doubt.

Speaking of defying the odds, we have all heard of parents who encourage kids with disabilities to accomplish the impossible. There is a story of Dan Mancina—a blind person who is a skateboard champion. Mat Armitage—the first amputee to compete on the show, American Ninja Warrior. If anyone has a right to live in self-doubt it is someone in such extenuating circumstances. Instead, these inspiring souls choose to stand in their own power and strength. Sure, it involves a lot of other things like hard work and dedication, but if you believe you can accomplish the impossible, chances are you will find ways to make it happen.

So how do we go from a doubter to a believer mindset? Let's break it down with the 3 As.

AWARENESS

The first step to any change is awareness. Awareness comes from self-reflection and asking yourself some important questions like:

1. Are you aware of how doubt holds you back from accomplishing your dreams?
2. How often do you see this play out in your life?
3. What could you accomplish if you believed in yourself?
4. Do you doubt yourself so much that you drive yourself into a frenzy of panic and anxiety?
5. Does it only come up at certain times or certain circumstances?

Write down instances where you think doubt held you back from trying something new or showing up bigger in your life. It is important to become aware of the patterns that rule our lives. They give us clues to what's holding us back.

Example
When I began running for the first time as an adult, I had so much doubt in myself. I thought I would never be able to run a mile. This doubt held me back from trying for a long time. I made up stories in my head. I avoided signing up for 5Ks, and I did whatever I could to make excuses. But somewhere deep down I also felt stuck and wanted to overcome this doubt. It wasn't until a friend of mine challenged me to think differently about it. She said I could run a mile that very day if I wanted to.

I said there was no way I could do it, but she slowed down my pace to an almost walking pace. She said I should focus on my breath and keep going until I hit a mile. At this point, I realized that it wasn't the idea of running a mile that seemed doubtful. It was the pressure I put on myself to run at a respectable pace that made me doubt myself.

ACCEPTANCE

Now that you have identified the patterns that hold you back, let's work on acceptance. While society has done a fantastic job of celebrating perfection and dismissing shortcomings, it is imperative that we accept the behavior that we are going to change. If we were not born doubting then it means that we have learned this trait. It is time to accept it without judgment and unlearn the old patterns. The way to acceptance is through detachment, courage, and compassion. You are working on an identity shift, so let's reframe the old story and work on creating a new one.

Example
Once I accepted the reality that I could run a mile, even if it was super slow, the acceptance kicked in. I also saw that doubting myself was holding me back from trying to break through the barrier. Once I saw myself do it, I began to believe in my own potential. I got inspired to educate myself on the skill required to increase my pace.

ACTION

Now that you have accepted that you tend to be a doubter more often than not, it is time to flip that thought on its head and declare that you are a BELIEVER and act like one. Believers take the leap and build their wings on the way down. In order to become a true believer, you have to have unbounded faith in yourself. Ask yourself what would a believer do in your situation. Would they second guess themselves or have an action plan ready? Start with a small step, one that doesn't paralyze you with fear. Something simple that will give you a sense of accomplishment at the end of the day. Look back at your day and find a win—no matter how big or small—and celebrate it. As you overcome smaller doubts in your day, you will feel empowered to try bigger things. Good things come to those who believe.

The good news about belief is that it can be created or shifted in an instant. All you need is a moment of inspiration to believe in yourself. One simple moment. Think about a time when you got inspired to sign up for a 5K run or ask your boss for a raise or spoke up against something that didn't feel right. Chances are something or someone inspired you in an instant, and you began the journey to do it. We are all a product of our conditioning, so it is important to know who you surround yourself with. If you are surrounded by others who inspire you to defy the odds, you probably do the same. But if you're surrounded by naysayers and doubters, you will probably develop the same doubts about yourself. We teach our children to fit into a mold

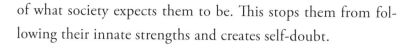

of what society expects them to be. This stops them from following their innate strengths and creates self-doubt.

Example

The day I ran my first mile, I couldn't deny it anymore. I accomplished something by letting go of my self-doubt for just one run. At the end of it, I had solid proof that I could run a mile. I felt empowered from the action I took in a moment of belief. It fueled my desire to improve my speed, and I worked on the tips and tools to get me there.

Summary

Doubt will keep us playing small. It prevents us from taking chances and getting creative. Doubt limits our potential. When we make the transition from doubter to believer, we open ourselves up to receive so much more. We take shots that might help us achieve what we once thought was impossible.

Affirmations to bring out your inner warrior.

WITCH (DOUBTER)
I will mess this up for sure.

WARRIOR (BELIEVER)
I will give it my best shot.

WITCH (DOUBTER)
Either I win, or I fail.

WARRIOR (BELIEVER)
Every attempt and effort is a win.

WITCH (DOUBTER)
I doubt I'll be able to do this.

WARRIOR (BELIEVER)
I believe I can do this.

WITCH (DOUBTER)
I am a DOUBTER.

WARRIOR (BELIEVER)
I am a BELIEVER.

The journey from doubter to believer starts with faith.

Let's Get to Work

RATE YOURSELF FROM 1 (DOUBTER) TO 5 (BELIEVER)

5

4

BELIEVER
mindset ON

3

Taking ACTION
and building the faith
muscle

2

ACCEPTANCE
and willingness to make
changes

1

AWARE or
becoming aware of the
tendency to be
a doubter

**THE JOURNEY FROM DOUBTER
TO BELIEVER**

Being a **DOUBTER**
and missing out on
opportunities

Where does doubter mindset shows up for you?

_____

_____

Where do you think you are on the above scale?

_____

_____

List 1 thing that holds you back from being a believer?

_____

_____

What is 1 thing you can do to become a believer?

_____

_____

What would being a believer do for you?

_____

_____

8

Fearless Not Fearful

You have two choices. To conquer your fear or to let your fear conquer you.

Roy T. Bennett

Fear is a conditioned belief. Our ancestors needed fear to anticipate danger to their lives. They relied on it for their daily survival. In this day and age, however, we live a safe and secure life. We don't need fear to protect us from our surroundings. If we pause to analyze our fears, most of them are irrational and unnecessary. They are likely holding us back from playing big in our lives, and those are the fears we want to effectively tackle.

What Is A Fearful Mindset?

A fearful mindset is something that we develop as we learn to keep up with the world around us. While a certain amount of fear can keep us safe, most of our fears are a result of our experiences and conditioning. Maybe you were expected to perform at a certain level as a child and felt that pressure. Maybe you were mocked when you attempted to do something out of your comfort zone. You probably developed a fear of making mistakes. Every time an opportunity presented itself, you worried about failing. A fearful mindset keeps us from living out our true potential and keeps us playing small.

What Is A Fearless Mindset?

A fearless mindset is something we need to train ourselves for. Being fearless doesn't mean having no fear. It means experiencing the fear and moving past it regardless. People who seem fearless have worked on their inner dialogue for years. They also likely had a team of cheerleaders along the way to help them face their fears. The ultimate goal of a fearless mindset is to help us bring out all those big dreams that we don't dare to share. So how do we accomplish all the amazing things we want to but cannot because of fear? Let's break it down.

Awareness

As always, the first step is to become aware of the fear as it comes up. How do we identify fear? Sometimes, fear can be evident in the form of a person or object. Other times, fear can be intrinsic stemming from our thoughts and imaginations. . We often like to control our environment as much as possible, so that we don't have to go out of our comfort zone and deal with fearful situations. We may use control as a facade to mask fear. We also see resistance in ourselves when we are put in a situation where the outcome may not be predictable. We resist change and progress because of fear. Take a look at where you feel frustrated or stuck in your life and assess whether it is fear that's holding you back. As you begin to observe the patterns in your life, you will become more aware of your deepest, darkest fear. This awareness is the first step in setting you free.

Example

Even though Maya put in a lot of effort at work, someone else always took credit for it. This created feelings of negativity in her. However, she wasn't typically a negative person. This upset her, and she couldn't figure out why she was feeling jealous of her colleagues. She began tracking her patterns and writing them down every time this happened.

As she tracked her experience, she realized that she didn't get credit for her work because she never spoke up or shared her work with confidence. She was fearful that if she claimed credit for her work, she would be pushed into the limelight. Deep down that triggered her fear of success. As she dove deeper into her behavior patterns, she noticed that she felt uneasy right after (timing) her colleagues got recognized for the work she had done. While the trigger was a feeling of being taken advantage of, the underlying fear was the fear of success.

ACCEPTANCE

Acceptance is a huge part of changing behavior. We can be aware of fear popping up every time we try to do something big but accepting that we have a fearful mindset in any situation will help us break free from it more effectively. Whether you are afraid to fail a test, speak up at work, set boundaries in a relationship, or get a divorce, you know in your heart that fear only does two things:

1. It holds you captive in your current situation.
2. It keeps you worrying about the past or future.

Most of our fears are usually recurring patterns in our lives. However, if we see them as a result of our conditioning and not a negative personality trait then it becomes a little easier to accept them. Facing our fears is one of the hardest things we can do, but it can also be the most liberating. And we all deserve to feel free and fearless in our pursuits. Try to visualize your life without the grip this fear has on you and be kind to yourself as you work your way out of it.

Acceptance Mantra: I accept that I am fearful, and I know that it's not my fault.

Example
When Maya realized that her feelings of jealousy were coming from a place of fear and not judgment toward her peers, she felt a sense of relief. She was able to look back at her child-hood and remember an instance when she was teased by her friends for forgetting her lines in a school play. This experience conditioned her to believe that if she showed up in front of an audience, she will be made fun of. By finding the origin of her fear, she had better insight and was able to accept that she was trained to be fearful.

ACTION

It is not easy to get rid of fear unless you have an experience that changes your perception of it. The best antidote to fear is action. The action doesn't have to be massive. It can be a small but brave step toward dispelling fear. Once you take ANY action, no matter how small, you will get your first glimpse of courage, and that will take you to the next step.

Let's take a look at some steps to becoming fearless. Once you assess the fear, it's time to decide how you will tackle it. You have two choices:

1. Take a leap of faith and do what scares you in one big action. For example, if you are afraid of skydiving but want to push your limits then a leap of faith (literally) may help you get over the fear.

2. Ease into it with baby steps until you are free of the fear. For example, if you have a fear of public speaking, you can start by speaking in front of a small and safe crowd like your family or close friends. Remember that Rome wasn't built in a day and neither was your fearful mindset. Breaking through a deep fear may require more patience than you think, so be kind to yourself as you work on peeling layers behind any fear.

One of the tricks I have used when I fear something is to imagine the situation, play it out in my mind in detail, and make peace with the worst-case scenario. Once you do that, any outcome will be better than you imagine. Changing our behavior is hard work and letting go of old patterns and beliefs around fear is uncomfortable. Acknowledge your efforts along the way.

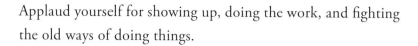

Applaud yourself for showing up, doing the work, and fighting the old ways of doing things.

Example

Maya decided to take baby steps and work her way to release the fear. She shared her fear with one of her coworkers and asked for help. They decided that, in the next meeting, her coworker would nudge her if she saw Maya struggling to speak up or take credit for her work. With some practice, Maya was able to show up as an expert during staff meetings.

Summary

A fearful mindset can be hidden behind a mask, and it will paralyze us and stop us from attempting even the smallest of tasks. When we become aware of it, accept it, and take action to challenge it, we become empowered to do more. A fearless mindset will take us to heights our fearful mindset couldn't even imagine.

Fear paralyzes and action liberates.

Affirmations to bring out your inner warrior.

WITCH (FEARFUL)
This is too scary.

WARRIOR (FEARLESS)
Is it as scary as I think?

WITCH (FEARFUL)
I can't do this.

WARRIOR (FEARLESS)
What happens if I try?

WITCH (FEARFUL)
I need to run back to safety.

WARRIOR (FEARLESS)
It would be amazing to overcome this.

WITCH (FEARFUL)
I am FEARFUL.

WARRIOR (FEARLESS)
I am FEARLESS.

The journey from fearful to fearless starts with action.

Let's Get to Work

RATE YOURSELF FROM 1 (FEARFUL) TO 5 (FEARLESS)

5
      FEARLESS mode ON

4
      Taking ACTION and building faith

3
      ACCEPTANCE and willingness to make changes

2
      AWARE or becoming aware of fearful mindset

      THE JOURNEY FROM FEARFUL TO FEARLESS

1
Feeling FEARFUL and dreading all change

When does a fearful mindset show up for you?

_____

_____

Where do you think you are on the above scale?

_____

_____

List 1 thing that holds you back from being in fearless mode?

_____

_____

What is 1 thing you can do to get to fearless mode?

_____

_____

What would being in fearless mode do for you?

_____

_____

9

Victor Not Victim

> Where there is a will, there is a way.
>
> *Albert Einstein*

What Is A Victim Mindset?

A victim mindset is one where you find something or someone to blame for your misfortunes. If you find yourself constantly irritated or complaining and angry with the world, chances are you are dealing with a victim mindset. We all know someone who is going through life with this mindset. A victim will go through life feeling negative and angry and spread that negativity wherever he or she goes.

What Is A Victor Mindset?

A victor mindset is one where you believe that you will eventually be able to come out stronger no matter what the situation. It is a belief system, a core value. And once you build it, it will only enhance your life exponentially. A victor is unstoppable and will overcome the odds that most people struggle with. They inspire others with their actions.

Marie Forleo wrote a book called "Everything is figureoutable." In it she shares a story about her mother who embodies the victor mentality. She believes that if you roll up your sleeves and get in there, any problem is figureoutable. This is a classic example of a victor mindset. You can take what life gives you,

THE WARRIOR MINDSET

or you can roll up your sleeves and get to work trying to figure it out.

So how do we go from victim to victor? It starts with shifting our focus. What are we focusing on? Are we focused on who we can blame for what's going on in our life, or are we going to focus on how to get out of the situation we're in? Let us look at the 3 As in this scenario.

AWARENESS

The first step is to do a quick audit of your emotions to see where you show up in a victim mindset. This is a fairly common mindset most of us find ourselves in at some point in our lives. It is also important to know that we cannot change what we don't have awareness about. Take stock of the things that are not working out in your life, and check to see if you're playing the blame game.

Example
A friend of mine, let's call her Mary, always blamed her parents for not taking more interest in her life when she was a kid. She would often express how she could've done better in her career if her parents had pushed her harder in high school. She got married to a man who beat the odds in his family over and over again. He was the first to graduate college, first to travel overseas for work, and first to own a home. He didn't under-stand her mentality. After multiple passionate conversations, he showed her that his odds of making it were much slimmer than

69

hers. If he had blamed his parents instead of fighting back, he wouldn't have made it this far. She realized that she couldn't really blame her parents for not pushing her. She saw how this blame game was only delaying her success. This awareness was the impetus for change in her life.

ACCEPTANCE

Once you begin to notice patterns of victimhood in your life, you will likely experience some heavy resistance to change. After all, shifting your focus from blaming others to taking ownership requires a lot of humility. You may also find yourself paralyzed with indecision once you become aware of your need to play the victim. One of the ways to go into acceptance is to avoid harshly judging yourself for it. Look at it as the end of one chapter and the beginning of another. The 'old you' was used to playing the victim, but the 'new you' is a victor and can beat the odds in any situation. Acceptance comes from giving ourselves grace as we understand and accept the mindset pitfalls that have held us back.

Example

In Mary's case, she initially resisted the idea that she was playing the victim, but she also felt stuck in her progress. She had spent years believing that her parents didn't push her to do better in school. After talking to her husband, she was able to make a shift in her perspective. She realized that she could not go back and change the past or the way her parents raised her, so she had to accept where she was and take charge of the situation.

Her old beliefs tied to playing the victim were sabotaging her success. This immediately put her in 'action' mode.

ACTION

The beauty of having awareness about an old pattern is that we want to change it immediately. This is human nature. When we know better, we want to do better. Once you have accepted that you tend to get into victim mode, you will realize that you don't want to stay there any longer. The first action step is to set a goal or destination for the new you. If you didn't play the victim, where would you be? What would you be doing? Once you have a goal set for yourself, break it down into smaller bits and get cracking at them immediately. Remember to keep your eye on the prize. If the witch rears its head to bring you down, know that your inner warrior (the victor) is capable of putting her down. As you check off your list of accomplishments, please be sure to celebrate each step of the way. Every win counts—even the smallest ones.

Example

I am thrilled to report that my friend, Mary, enrolled herself in school, got her degree as a clinical social worker, and is following her passion to help domestically abused children. She no longer plays the victim and continues to be a role model for herself and her kids.

Summary

Playing victim will have us blaming everyone else for our problems, but once we make our way to victor mode, there is no stopping us. We become badass versions of ourselves who will stop at nothing to achieve our dreams. Victors take responsibility, get resourceful, and win against all odds.

Affirmations to bring out your inner warrior.

WITCH (VICTIM)
It's not my fault. I'm stuck.

WARRIOR (VICTOR)
How do I get out of this situation?

WITCH (VICTIM)
I blame (insert person or situation).

WARRIOR (VICTOR)
I am responsible for my future.

WITCH (VICTIM)
If only (insert person or situation) changed, I could be or do more.

WARRIOR (VICTOR)
I can accomplish anything I put my mind to.

WITCH (VICTIM)
I am a VICTIM.

WARRIOR (VICTOR)
I am a VICTOR.

The journey from victim to victor starts with focus.

Let's Get to Work

RATE YOURSELF FROM 1 (VICTIM) TO 5 (VICTOR)

5

VICTOR mode on
(Taking charge)

4

Taking ACTION and
shifting focus

3

ACCEPTANCE and
willingness to make
changes

2

AWARE or becoming
aware of tendency to
play victim

**THE JOURNEY FROM
VICTIM TO VICTOR**

1

Playing VICTIM
(consciously or
unconsciously)

Where does victim mindset show up for you?

Where do you think you are on the above scale?

List 1 thing that holds you back from being in Victor mode?

What is 1 thing you can do to get to Victor mode?

What would Victor mode do for you?

10

Secure Not Insecure

Confidence is not "they will like me." Confidence instead is I'll be fine if they don't."

Christina Grimmie

Insecurity may be one of the biggest things that come in the way of our success. Sometimes it brings out the worst in us. Once again, this is not an emotion we are born with. It is ingrained in us by society. We are taught from a young age that we need to be better than our peers whether it is at home, school, or on the playground. It is only natural that we see our success in comparison to others. But comparison, as we know, is the thief of joy.

We don't have to look far for inspiration. Just step out into your backyard or go for a walk in your neighborhood, and you will see that there are all kinds of flowers blooming next to each other. They're not trying to compete with each other. They're all competing for the sun and trying to reach as high as they can go. They don't shame each other or hide their growth from each other. They are secure in their path and happy to blossom near each other without feeling threatened. So why do we struggle so much with insecurity? We may be one of the most intelligent species on the planet, but we're also blessed (or cursed) with an ego. On the one hand, we can successfully eradicate deadly diseases using our brains, but on the other hand, we are slaves to our mindset.

What Is An Insecure Mindset?

An insecure mindset is one where we give in to the ego and operate from a place of lack. Insecurity can come from a place of low self-confidence, cultural or societal pressure, or even from being a perfectionist. When we are insecure about something, we become focused on one thing, which is to find a way to feel better about ourselves. Unfortunately, we will do anything to get there including, but not limited to, wishing ill on others.

What Is A Secure Mindset?

A secure mindset is one where we are confident in our strengths and weaknesses. We have had enough growth and maturity to know that there are certain things we are good at and others where we need to lean in for help. We are able to initiate the warrior whenever the ugly witch rears its head to bring up any insecurity. A secure mindset is an empowered and self-confident mindset. It embodies abundance, contentment, and a sense of collaboration over competition.

Journey From Insecure To Secure

While most of us are born secure and confident in our skin, we lose our way as we try to fit into this world. As we see those around us do well, we feel threatened and want to find any path to make us feel better. Most people are in denial about their insecurities, and we all have them in some way, shape, or form. As always, the first step is to become aware of our insecurities,

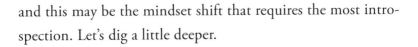

and this may be the mindset shift that requires the most intro-spection. Let's dig a little deeper.

AWARENESS

If we weren't born insecure then where did these feelings begin? Let's go back to our childhood, and see how and where it became difficult for you to fit in. Did you feel judged about the color of your skin, your physical appearance, or the way you spoke or behaved? Maybe you felt judged because of your lack of confidence or fear of judgement. Usually, our insecurities will follow a recurring pattern and be tied to fears instilled in us from childhood. Self-reflection is the best way to identify and become aware of our insecurities.

Example
My friend, Cynthia, is a middle child. Growing up, she always had to compete for attention with her siblings. She was always trying hard to please everyone and felt like she never succeeded. As she got older, this fear of competition was huge in her head. Without realizing what was happening, she compared herself to her peers all the time. She felt jealous of them as they suc-ceeded, and sometimes secretly wished that they failed, so she could succeed. The stress of this constant comparison did not allow her to enjoy her own success as she feared it was short-lived. With time, the stress began to multiply, and the anxiety got too much for her. We would talk about it all the time, and I found myself constantly trying to make her see how much she had accomplished. We began working on a gratitude list that

contained 3 things she was grateful. She would send me this list each night. As she began to see how blessed she was, she became aware of how much her insecurities were controlling her. She was embarrassed that her insecurity was the root of her anxiety and lack of gratitude. We talked about how this new awareness is the first step to rising above it.

ACCEPTANCE

Self-reflection is the cornerstone of security. The more we introspect and reflect on our behaviors, the more we can pinpoint the origin of our insecurity. If you feel insecure in one area of your life, you will not feel confident in that area. You may be tempted to avoid thinking about it, but the only way to grow out of it is to accept it. Remind yourself that insecurity is a product of our conditioning. Sometimes it helps to identify the cause of insecurities. Asking ourselves when was the first time our insecurity showed up is a good place to start. Here are some likely scenarios that you may have experienced:

1. Lack of confidence
2. Trying to fit in
3. Pursuit of perfection

Whatever it is, remember that insecurity is a response to one of the above stimuli. If you're going to blame anyone blame the stimuli. Once you take the embarrassment out of it, you can begin working on yourself to become more comfortable in your skin.

Example

For Cynthia, once it became obvious that she was operating from a place of insecurity, she knew she had to get over it. But her inner witch kept showing up to embarrass and shame her. Since this was a tough one for her, we worked on it one step at a time. We stopped celebrating the fact that she had narrowed down the problem. Now it would be much easier to accept it. She also connected the problem back to her childhood. After speaking to some childhood friends and some of her more recent friends, she realized that everyone around her thought she was intelligent, talented, and could accomplish anything she put her mind to. This came as a shock to her as her inner witch had convinced her that she wasn't good enough.

ACTION

Insecurities are like weeds. They have deep roots and like any aggressive weed, we have to constantly keep pulling them out until we get to the root. Otherwise, it will take over the whole garden. The inner witch will rear its ugly head whenever it can. But it is up to us to keep that inner witch at bay and bring out the warrior. So how do we combat insecurity? Here are some action steps to help:

1. Identify the root cause by talking to a trusted friend or professional.
2. Build a case for yourself. List out your strengths and accomplishments.

3. Always leave room for mistakes and imperfections. Show yourself compassion if you slip.
4. Practice asking for help and accepting it graciously when you need it.
5. Build your faith muscle. Remind yourself that you have come this far, and you can surely keep going.

Practice abundance and gratitude for the things that work in your favor.

Example

Once Cynthia realized that the inner witch had been controlling the narrative, she knew that it was time to initiate warrior mode. Together we made a list of all the badass things she had accomplished in her life. She wrote them down on a piece of paper and read the list out loud every day in front of the mirror with a huge smile. She realized that she never gave herself credit for the things she achieved as she was too focused on what she didn't have. She also noticed that when she didn't feel threatened, she actually was pretty inclusive and enjoyed the project more. She continued to make gratitude lists every day and began to feel a shift in her energy. Overtime, she was able to initiate warrior mode as soon as the anxiety began brewing and felt empowered to put the inner witch back in her place.

Summary

Insecurity is a state of mind that induces negative emotions like jealousy, envy, anger, and frustration. On the flip side, when we feel secure in our own skin, we know that each of us is born with a unique gift to serve the world. There is no competition. In fact, we are open to sharing and collaborating with like-minded individuals, so that we can grow together.

Affirmations to bring out your inner warrior.

WITCH (INSECURE)
I have to attend this event, or I may not get invited next time.

WARRIOR (SECURE)
I will skip it as I don't enjoy such events.
Maybe something better will come up.

WITCH (INSECURE)
Last time I spoke up, everyone laughed at me. I'm never taking that chance again.

WARRIOR (SECURE)
Even though it's hard to speak up, I know the only way to overcome it is to keep trying.

WITCH (INSECURE)
I can't tell anyone my idea, or they will steal it.

WARRIOR (SECURE)
Let them try. I have many more where those came from.

WITCH (INSECURE)
I have FOMO - (Fear of Missing Out).

WARRIOR (SECURE)
I have JOMO - (Joy of Missing Out).

WITCH (INSECURE)
I am INSECURE.

WARRIOR (SECURE)
I am SECURE.

The journey from insecure to secure starts with the self.

Let's Get to Work

RATE YOURSELF FROM 1 (INSECURE) TO 5 (SECURE)

5

SECURE
mindset
activated

4

Taking ACTION
and building trust

3

ACCEPTANCE
and willingness to make
changes

2

AWARE or
becoming aware of
insecure mindset

**THE JOURNEY FROM INSECURE
TO SECURE**

1

Feeling
INSECURE and
unable to trust

When does an insecure mindset show up for you?

_____

_____

Where do you think you are on the above scale?

_____

_____

List 1 thing that holds you back from being in a secure mindset?

_____

_____

What is 1 thing you can do to get to a secure mindset?

_____

_____

What would being in a secure mindset do for you?

_____

_____

11

Warrior Not Worrier

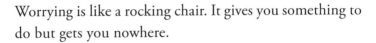

Worrying is like a rocking chair. It gives you something to do but gets you nowhere.

Glenn Turner

We are not born worriers, but based on our conditioning and taught responses, we develop the habit of worrying. The first step to breaking free of this habit is to identify where you are on the worry spectrum. A little worry is natural and warranted as you deal with the ups and downs of your life. But if worry begins to consume you to the point where you are getting stuck in a rut or unable to find your Zen again then you need to find ways to break free.

Worry is typically tied to negative emotions. We never worry about how good things can be; we worry about how bad things can be. While a situation may warrant worrying, the act of worrying doesn't provide any comfort. So instead of focusing on what could go wrong or what would happen if this wasn't your reality, why not focus on how to feel good despite the problematic situation you are in? The opposite of worry is faith. If you stop overworking your "worry" muscle and start working your "faith" muscle then you may just be able to find a way to break free of your thought patterns and find a way out of the situation you are in.

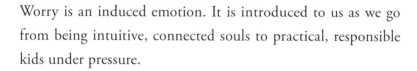

Worry is an induced emotion. It is introduced to us as we go from being intuitive, connected souls to practical, responsible kids under pressure.

My friend, Wendy, couldn't help but worry about her son's future when he was admitted to hospital with a head injury. Her mind would race with thoughts of whether he would recover fully, whether he would function normally, or develop a learning disability, etc.

How do we get into a warrior mindset so that no matter what life throws at us, we are ready to tackle it? Here are a few simple things to remember:

AWARENESS

If you're a worrier, you're probably caught up in a downward spiral with difficult situations. You also likely feel exhausted and depleted from all that worrying. Next time you catch yourself worrying and living in the "what if's," pause and remind yourself that there is another way. You cannot change what you are not aware of. Begin noticing your thoughts, and track how often you get caught up in the worry.

Example
In Wendy's case, once her mind went into this downward spiral, she struggled to break free. If her son spoke to her in the hospital, she couldn't interact with him because she was terrified of what would happen to him. It was when her son called her out on it that she realized that she was missing out on the precious

moments he was giving her. Worrying so much was making her live in the past or in the future and missing out on the present.

ACCEPTANCE

The second step is to accept that we are caught up in a state of worry. It's time to acknowledge your tendency to go into a worry spiral and accept that this may be a problem. This is usually an easy one to identify, and people are generally aware of whether they are worriers or warriors.

Example

In Wendy's case, as soon as her son made her aware of her worrying, she had no choice but to accept it. He was right. She had a tendency to worry in most situations. In identifying the behavior, she realized she got that from her dad and knew that there had to be another way.

ACTION

Once you realize that worrying is not a productive emotion, you will know that it's time to take action. But how do we avoid free falling into worry every time a dire situation presents itself? Follow these action steps:

1. Hit the brakes. As soon as you become aware that you are slipping into the worry void, hit the brakes to stop the thoughts.
2. Look at the facts. Are your worry thoughts true? Or is that way of thinking based on your deepest fears?

3. What is the worst-case scenario? Imagine and make peace with the worst-case scenario then work toward the best-case scenario.
4. Flip the script. It is likely what you worry about might happen, but it is also likely that the opposite might happen.
5. Control what you can. It is not easy to stop worrying in some cases, but if you focus on what you can control, it will make things easier.
6. Find your people. Who can help you talk through the worry? How can you reach someone for help?

Example
In Wendy's case, she knew that she was only thinking of the worst-case scenario with her son, and that's what sent her spiraling. She decided to evaluate her thoughts and eliminate false assumptions. As she got out of the downward spiral, she felt gratitude for the moments of joy she had when he awoke. She also decided that instead of worrying about him, she could focus on reliving some of their favorite childhood memories and even plan for some future ones.

SUMMARY

Worry keeps us from getting ahead. It limits our growth and success. It keeps us from believing in and exploring the magic of the world. When we do the work to go from worrier to warrior, we allow ourselves to live a full, joyful life filled with endless possibilities.

Affirmations to bring out your inner warrior.

WORRIER
What if things went horribly wrong?

WARRIOR
I can only control my actions and reactions.

WORRIER
Things always go wrong for me.

WARRIOR
Everything happens for a reason.

WORRIER
I worry about the future.

WARRIOR
Worry isn't helping me. Let me talk to someone.

WORRIER
I am a WORRIER.

WARRIOR
I am a WARRIOR.

The journey from worrier to warrior starts with analysis.

Let's Get to Work

RATE YOURSELF FROM 1 (WORRIER) TO 5 (WARRIOR)

5

4

WARRIOR
mode on

3

Taking ACTION
towards what is
in our control

2

ACCEPTANCE
and willingness to
make changes

1

AWARE or
becoming aware of
tendency to be a
worrier

THE JOURNEY FROM WORRIER
TO WARRIOR

Living in Worrier mode
aka past or future

Where does worrier mindset shows up for you?

Where do you think you are on the above scale?

List 1 thing that holds you back from being in Warrior mode?

What is 1 thing you can do to get to Warrior mode?

What would being in Warrior mode do for you?

Summary

Win the mind, win the world

These seven mindset shifts will help you detox and clean out your mind. Decluttering the mind will give you clarity, free up space for more, and attract new beginnings.

Let's summarize what we learned in this book.

1. **Mindset is everything.** Our mindset controls our thoughts, words, and actions, which in turn influence the results we see in our lives. So, if there is anything sacred and holy in our body, it is the 6 inches between our ears. Win the mind, win your life.

2. **The Witch and the Warrior.** Let us acknowledge and accept that we have both, the witch and the warrior, sitting on each side of our mind. One is trying to pull us down and the other is trying to help us fly. Ask yourself, "What would the Warrior do?

3. **A reality check.** Take a bird's eye view of life's journey, and you will see that the definition of success defined by society isn't always the best for us. Sometimes in our

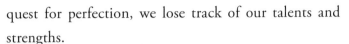

quest for perfection, we lose track of our talents and strengths.

4. **The seven mindset shifts.** Once you have been through the seven mindset shifts, identify how and where the witch shows up in your mind, follow the 3 steps (awareness, acceptance, and action) to do the work to empower the warrior within, and put the evil witch in her place.

5. **Celebrate every win.** Take a moment to congratulate yourself on not only identifying limitations that have held you back but also taking pride in the fact that you committed to doing the work to release those limiting mindsets.

6. **Time for the "new" you:** As you shed old beliefs and patterns, you will be able to see your true authentic self emerge. This "new" you is ready to take on the challenges of the world in full warrior mode.

7. **Get ready for an energetic elevation.** Once you have done the inner work and gained some mastery of the mindset, you will release negative emotions and feel lighter. Your energy will vibrate at a higher frequency. This will help you attract what you desire with ease.

Conclusion

Knowledge is not power, awareness is power, and action is a superpower

If you succeeded in implementing the 3 As and managed to free yourself of the old conditioning to create a shift, then I applaud your efforts and congratulate you on taking action toward creating significant change. I know it's not easy and takes a lot of inner work.

Not only did you do the introspective work and get real with yourself, but you gave yourself grace, and came out better and stronger for it. You fought your old conditioning and created new neural pathways by interrupting the status quo.

As you begin to unleash your inner warrior, you will see a shift in how you experience life. You will become more confident in your skin and stand a little taller in your own power. As you begin to do that you will automatically shine your light a little brighter paving the way for those around you to shine their light too.

Taming the inner witch and unleashing your inner warrior will have incredibly positive changes in your life. Here are a few things you may experience:

1. You save time and energy that you used to spend in worry, fear, lack, or insecurity.
2. You embrace yourself as you are and have a heightened awareness of your strengths.
3. You think of creative solutions to problems as you are not caught in your own stories.
4. You attract people and experiences that are positive and uplifting.
5. You can see these patterns in others and show them compassion.
6. You gain confidence in yourself and begin to dream bigger.
7. You become more intuitive as you declutter your mind.

Now, let's take a moment to celebrate some victories.

You did it!
You put the witch in her place and brought out your inner warrior.

You made the shift from stressed to blessed, scarcity to abundance, doubter to believer, fearful to fearless, victim to victor, insecure to secure, and worrier to warrior.

The only thing left to do is to pay it forward and share the joy you receive from elevating your mindset. Start with your family, friends, and your community. Who do you know that could benefit from this knowledge?

Welcome to the new you. Warrior on, my friend!

Acknowledgments

The list of people I need to thank for making this book possible is endless but I will attempt to share my gratitude.

This book is in your hands with the support of the following people.

My family and my friends for all their support.

My intuitive friends and teachers who pushed me through my fears.

My mom, who instilled in me the positive beliefs and faith that led to the discovery of the warrior mindset.

You, the reader, who is ready to unleash the warrior within and win the world and perhaps needed a nudge in the right direction.

My curiosity which led me down the rabbit hole of doing a 'Ph.D. in me' and realized that mindset truly holds the power to change our thoughts, words, and actions.

My struggles which gave me a reason to pursue answers and solutions. They gave me the insight I needed to discover this truth.

My ADD brain which requires things to be simplified and broken down to be understood. It gave me the clarity in creating the structure of this book.

Technology, which made it easy to do research or pen down thoughts as and when they came to me.

And finally my publishing company, who held my hand through the scary publishing world.

I am humbled and honored to play the smallest role in helping you unleash the warrior inside.

I'd love to hear your feedback, so please feel free to send me a note via my social media handles listed below.

INSTAGRAM

Instagram:
https://www.instagram.com/
mindbodyspiritwarrior/

FACEBOOK

Facebook:
https://www.facebook.com/
FitWarriorLife/

LINKEDIN

LinkedIn:
https://www.linkedin.com/in/
fitwarriorlife/

Resources

When you go through each of the mindset shifts, you will have an opportunity to rate yourself on a scale of 1-5. That is, 1 (victim) to 5 (victor) on each one and see which one you need to work on first.

For an online printable version, please click copy and paste this link in your web browser: https://www.fitwarriorlife.com/bookresources or scan the QR Code on this page.

BOOK RESOURCES

If you rate yourself close to 5 in any of the mindsets, I applaud you and give you a virtual high five. You have done some work to rise above the low-vibe mindset blocks.

If you are closer to 1 on any of them then you have some work to do. But you are not alone. Try to give yourself time and some grace to make the transition. Focus on the changes you are making and celebrate every win, no matter how small.

Rome wasn't built in a day. You didn't acquire these mindsets in a day, and you won't recover from them in a day. If you go to my website (https://www.fitwarriorlife.com/bookresources) or scan the QR code shown on this page, you will see other resources to help in the journey. Remember that the journey of personal development is a lifelong one. While it may feel like you have overcome the mindset pitfalls, they may sneak in when you least expect them to. But you can always go back to your toolbox (this book) and take the microphone away from the witch. She only has power when you hand her the mic. Remember you are always in charge. Own your power, keep reminding yourself of it, and shine your light so bright that others are inspired to shine too.

YouTube: Another resource that may help you connect with your mindset is my new YouTube channel, which you can find on this link

https://www.youtube.com/@FITWARRIORLIFE
or scan the QR code below.

YOUTUBE

Bonus: Another big benefit of working on your mindset is that you can go from feeling the fear of missing out to the joy of missing out. Please see the QR code below for more.

FOMO TO JOMO

Thank You

Thank You For Reading My Book!

I really appreciate all of your feedback, and I love hearing what you have to say.

I need your input to make the next version of this book and my future books even better.

Please leave me a helpful review on Amazon letting me know what you thought of the book.

Thank you so much!
Chitra Rochlani

Made in the USA
Columbia, SC
21 November 2024

29b37e88-1a7a-4545-90d5-d74fe26ce171R01